Grammar

KINGFISHER
NEW YORK

Text and design copyright © Toucan Books Ltd. 2011
Based on an original concept by Toucan Books Ltd.
Illustrations copyright © Simon Basher 2011

Published in the United States by Kingfisher,
175 Fifth Ave., New York, NY 10010
Kingfisher is an imprint of Macmillan Children's Books, London.
All rights reserved.

Consultant: Orin K. Hargraves

Designed and created by Basher
www.basherbooks.com

Dedicated to Michelle and Rufus

Distributed in the U.S. and Canada by Macmillan, 175 Fifth Ave.,
New York, NY 10010

Library of Congress Cataloging-in-Publication data has been applied for.

ISBN 978-0-7534-6596-7

Kingfisher books are available for special promotions and premiums.
For details contact: Special Markets Department, Macmillan, 175 Fifth
Ave., New York, NY 10010.

For more information, please visit www.kingfisherbooks.com

Printed in China
9 8 7 6 5 4
4TR/0216/WKT/UG/128MA

CONTENTS

Introduction
Grammar

Let's hear it for the champions of the word world, the grammar gang. Stick with these guys, kids, and you'll soon learn your way around a sentence. It's a high-class beat that doesn't get enough attention in today's rough-and-tumble backstreets of tweets and text messages. This error-busting bunch has been policing parts of speech for centuries, and there's not a verb form gone bad or an incomplete sentence slouching around inside a paragraph today that can slip anything past them.

Okay, okay, so grammar has a bad rep. You might think it's just a set of good-for-nothing rules, made up by evil English teachers who get their kicks by giving their red pens a workout. Not so. Words are a feisty mob of scrappers—all set to rough up your sentences unless this crew is there to put them in their proper place. You see, that's their job—making sure words toe the line and express ideas with clarity and completeness. It's a tough task, though, and they could sure use some rookies to help them out. That's where you come in. Hey, what are you waiting for? Let's meet this gang.

Punctuation

* The earliest punctuation marks date from ancient Greece
* Originally used to help actors deliver their lines properly
* Latin *punctuare* means "to mark with points or dots"

Grammar and I need each other. Built into the very fabric of written text, we complement each other and make a whole. Either one of us is meaningless without the other; together, our power is immense!

I help grammar shape a strong body of meaning. You can find me nestling between clauses, nudging apart phrases, and securely snapped to the end of a sentence. When a president reads a historic speech and sees the small curved mark known as a comma, he pauses, adding dramatic effect to his words. Great actresses look to us for direction—exclamation points make them gasp in shock, while question marks cause them to furrow their beautiful brows in uncertainty! And we all know what parents mean when they say, "No. Period."

✓ **DO** use commas to separate words and groups of words when they form a list: *We saw elephants, tigers, lions, and chimpanzees at the zoo.*

✗ **DON'T** use a comma to separate a subject from its verb: *My favorite backpack split at the seams* (NOT *My favorite backpack, split at the seams*).

Punctuation

Chapter 1
What's the Word?

There's no time for slackers in the word world, and these eager beavers won't let you down! Here to serve you and your ideas, this crew gets to work the minute you start to put your thoughts into writing. First off, Noun and Verb get together to sketch out an initial idea, while Adjective and Adverb do all the describing. Then Prepositions and Conjunctions jump in to connect it all together. And, presto, you've got yourself a sentence! It's all about being understood, and these industrious dudes are working flat out to make everything clear. Let's hear what they have to say . . .

Noun

Verb

Tense

Pronoun

Adjective

Adverb

Prepositions

Conjunctions

Article

Noun

■ What's the Word?

✸ The subject or an object of a sentence
✸ Performs the action of the verb in an active sentence
✸ In a passive sentence, receives the action of the verb

What's the word? I am the word and the word is I!
I am the star of a sentence, and all the other words
simply add to my wonderfulness. They sometimes call
me a "subject," but I prefer "ruler," for I am the very
person, place, thing, or idea that a sentence is all about.

*Chocolate, velvet, goblins, ponies, a tarantula, Martians,
melodies, rubies,* and *an elephant*—boy, am I into *things*!
If you can see, hear, taste, or touch me, I'm a concrete
noun. When I'm a feeling or a thought that you can't
exactly hold (think *boredom, anger,* or *sleepiness*), I'm an
abstract noun. I can also be a proper noun—a name, a
place, a day of the week—with a capital initial letter.
And when I'm feeling super intelligent, I'm a compound
noun, made up of two or more words: smarty-pants!

✓ **DO** capitalize the first letter of a person's profession when it is used as part of their title: *Dr. Smith*.

✗ **DON'T** capitalize when speaking of a person's profession in general: *Anne's dad is a doctor at the city hospital.*

Noun

Verb
■ What's the Word?

* A word that expresses an action, condition, or state of being
* Changes to show who is doing the action: *I go*, *he goes*
* Uses tense to indicate time—past, present, or future

You want action? I provide it. I really set things in motion. Without me, Noun would never go anywhere or do anything. A bike (noun) is nice . . . but without me there's no hope of *jumping* on that bike and *pedaling* it down the street. You see, a bike's no fun unless you can *ride* it. You can count on me to make things happen.

I'm verbally distinguished, too, for I have two voices: the active and the passive. I use the active when the subject of a sentence is performing the action of the verb: *My dog stole the pizza slice off my plate*. And I use the passive when the subject of a sentence is having the action of the verb done to it: *My pizza slice was stolen*. "Stole" or "was stolen"—whichever way you look at it, no sentence is complete unless I'm right in the thick of it.

✓ **DO** use the active voice for greater impact: *Larry kicked the ball straight at the goalkeeper* (NOT *The ball was kicked straight at the goalkeeper by Larry*).

✗ **DON'T** avoid the passive voice completely. It can be useful if the doer of an action is unknown: *I had a nasty feeling that I was being watched by someone*.

Verb

Tense

■ What's the Word?

✳ Derives from the Middle English word for "time": *tens*
✳ Indicates a shift in time from one action or state to another
✳ Shown by changing the verb form: *he did*, *she does*

Tense? It can be! There's no denying it, we words have to stick together. Noun can't *move* without Verb, and without me, Verb would be stuck in some awful time vacuum—for Sentence has chosen me to show when talk is of the past, the present, or the future. Yes, I am Sentence's great timekeeper.

Sure, Verb is a great doer, but I'm the one who says exactly when all this activity occurs: Grandma's chili *was* too fiery (past tense); she *knows* who is to blame (present tense); he *will pay* for it (future tense)! I spell it out by adding helping (AKA auxiliary) words (like "will" to express the future of "pay") and by special verb forms known as inflections. In *Grandma drank a gallon of water*, "drank" is the inflected form of "drink." It can all get very "in-tense"!

✓ **DO** change tenses to indicate a shift in time from one action or state to another: *The children are proud of the Christmas tree, which they decorated themselves.*

✗ **DON'T** change tenses if the time frame for each action or state is the same: *After work my father came home, changed into his sweats, and exercised.*

Tense

Pronoun
What's the Word?

* Handy little word that substitutes for an overworked noun
* Stops nouns from repeating themselves
* Often follows established rules of gender and case

Given the slightest chance, Noun hogs the limelight, but there's more than one celebrity of the word world: I'm talking about *me*, of course. Like a stunt double for a movie star, I stand in for hotshot Noun and, gee, am I good!

Instead of *Jenna's dog, Bruno, ate Jenna's homework and Jenna is in big trouble*, I give you *Jenna's dog, Bruno, ate* her *homework and* she *is in big trouble*. Sounds easy, but this job requires flexibility. In my personal form, I replace the subject or object of a sentence: *he/him, she/her*. In my reflexive form, I refer back to the subject: *himself, herself, itself*. But I can also be demonstrative: *this* and *that*, and interrogative: *who?* or *what?* And, boy, can I be possessive . . . but more of that in chapter 3, where I get you all to *myself* once more!

✓ **DO** remember that personal, reflexive, and possessive pronouns must agree in terms of gender: *Danny can get his own breakfast; Susan contradicted herself.*

✗ **DON'T** forget that most pronouns change according to case—that is, whether they are the subject of a sentence (*he, she, they*) or the object (*him, her, them*).

Pronoun

Adjective

What's the Word?

* Tells all there is to know about a noun or a pronoun
* Usually comes before the noun in a sentence: a *red* car
* Can be used to liven up an otherwise dull story

I'm a descriptive genius; I just live for the nitty-gritty. Noun boasts about being a star, but looks and personality are all up to me. Take a plain and simple Noun like *toast*, for example. "Yum," you might think . . . but what about *cold* toast, or *wet* toast, or *blackened, scorched* toast? Still tempted? I tell it like it is— right down to the smallest detail. Got the picture?

Adjective

✓ **DO** capitalize adjectives that are formed from proper nouns: *the American flag; some Mexican food; an African soccer player.*

✗ **DON'T** confuse an adjective with an adverb: *your nose smells bad* (adjective) is quite different from *your nose smells badly* (adverb)!

Adverb

What's the Word?

- ✸ A word that tells you more about a verb
- ✸ Usually comes after the verb in a sentence: I ran *quickly*
- ✸ Helps the stories you tell move from fuzzy to focused

Adverb

I'm a word detective. I tease and test Verb, probing for just a little bit more information. You slept last night, you say? Don't keep me in the dark—exactly how did you sleep? *Deeply* or *fitfully*? *Peacefully* or *restlessly*? I'm easy to spot, since I end mostly in "ly." I don't like to come before the verb in a sentence, but you'll see me make an appearance *eventually*.

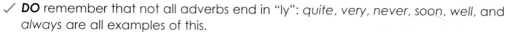

✓ **DO** remember that not all adverbs end in "ly": *quite, very, never, soon, well,* and *always* are all examples of this.

✗ **DON'T** forget that it is not always a good idea to split infinitives when using adverbs: *I asked Bob to speak quietly indoors* (NOT *I asked Bob to quietly speak indoors*).

Prepositions
■ What's the Word?

✳ Take their name from the Latin meaning "placed in front of"
✳ Explain how nouns relate to other parts of a sentence
✳ Always come before a noun in a sentence

We're a bunch of twitchy little operators who explain the connection between Noun or Pronoun and the rest of a sentence. With us on the job, you'll never be lost in space, because we're the guys who help Verb pin down where whatever happens, happens.

Imagine trying to get a bad-tempered donkey into a stable. Whoops! That shaggy-haired, ornery burro (noun) starts a-kicking. But where are those kicks landing? If the angry brute is kicking *against* the barn door, then you'll have to call the carpenter, but if she's beating *upon* your thigh, or hammering *at* your rear end, it's an SOS to the doctor! And if you're riding *on* the little donkey, be careful you don't end up *beneath* the beast, flat *on* the ground, just waiting for her to trample all *over* you!

✓ **DO** make sure you use the objective case with pronouns after prepositions: *Mom gave the candy to Stevie and me* (NOT *Stevie and I*).

✗ **DON'T** use a preposition when you don't need one: *Where is it?* (NOT *Where's it at?*).

Prepositions

Conjunctions

What's the Word?

- Nifty words that join two clauses or nouns together
- Coordinating conjunctions include *and*, *but*, *or*, *so*
- Sometimes come in pairs: *either/or*, *not only/but also*

Like our buddies the Preps, we're tiny little things that you don't always notice in a sentence—and that's how we like it. We are strong, silent types . . .

Just like engineers building a bridge, we span across a sentence connecting one phrase or clause to the next. Without us, you'd end up talking like a robot. Like this: *I love going to school on my skateboard. Mom thinks that it's dangerous. She knows that I'm pretty good. She worries that I might fall.* No, no, no! You love going to school on your skateboard, *but* your Mom worries that it's too dangerous. She knows you are pretty good at it, *although* she still worries that you might fall. That's better! We also let you weigh possibilities—whether to eat *not only* pizza, *but also* cherry pie. Go for it!

✓ **DO** put a comma before the coordinating conjunction when joining independent clauses: *Tom scored three goals, and his friends were impressed.*

✗ **DON'T** begin a sentence with a conjunction: *Sally had an omelet for lunch, but she didn't like it* (NOT *Sally had an omelet for lunch. But she didn't like it*).

Conjunctions

Article

■ What's the Word?

☀ Used to refer to nouns: *the* solar system; *an* asteroid
☀ "The" always refers to a specific object: *the* moon
☀ Less-specific or unidentified objects use "a": *a* star

Oh yes! Oh yes! Give it up for the maestro. I am the champ, believe me—the word most often used in the English language. Not just any one, but "the" one.

You'll know my twin, too: "a." We do the same job, but we couldn't be more different from each other. I am the definite article: I know what I want and make sure I get it by pointing to particulars: I want *the* hat in *the* shop over there, and I want it now; or, I'm thirsty, pass me *the* soda on *the* kitchen table. Meanwhile, sibling "a" is the indefinite article. Head in the clouds, "a" just imagines what might be nice: I'd like *a* hat—any hat would do; Or, *a* soda would be nice right now. It's not difficult to tell us apart: I'm specific; she's abstract—with me, it's not What's "a" word? but What's "the" word!

✓ **DO** use "a" before words that begin with a consonant sound and use "an" before words that begin with a vowel sound: *a pear, an apple*.

✗ **DON'T** use "a" before words beginning with a silent "h" (*herb, hour, honest*): *Parsley is an herb; it's been an hour since she left; he's an honest guy.*

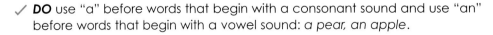

Article

Chapter 2
Team Sentence

Time to practice your writing skills with Team Sentence. Boy, these guys are smart! They train hard, support one another, and bring their own skills to the game. A team of superstars, there are no egos here. Simple Sentence and Syntax keep a tight rein on content and structure, while Clause and Phrase fill in the details. Incomplete Sentence and Run-on Sentence can take the game in the wrong direction. They mean well, but they disrupt the flow at times. Thankfully, Complex Sentence is there to get them back on track. Together, these players make an impressive lineup. Let's see 'em in action.

Simple
Sentence

Syntax

Clause

Phrase

Incomplete
Sentence

Run-on
Sentence

Complex
Sentence

Simple Sentence
■ Team Sentence

※ The basic building block of written and spoken language
※ Must contain a subject and its verb
※ Can be a statement, question, command, or exclamation

I'm Team Sentence's central player when it comes to expressing thoughts and ideas. I'm a solid, no-nonsense kind of guy. Don't come to me for fancy footwork and flashy skills—what you see is what you get!

I keep my eye on the basics and make sure a subject and its verb are always present and correct. Noun is the subject of a sentence—that's who or what the sentence is about—while Verb leaps into action to tell you what Noun is up to. Together, they express a complete thought, and a sentence just isn't a sentence if that's missing. Sometimes you might find two of me appearing on either side of a conjunction to make a compound sentence. *Get to know me better*, and *you'll see me everywhere*. It's as simple as that!

✓ **DO** remember to start every sentence with a capital letter and end it with a period, question mark, or exclamation point: *What did he say? I don't believe it!*

✗ **DON'T** forget that the subject does not always have to be stated: *Stop teasing your brother!* (The understood subject is "you.")

Simple Sentence

Syntax
■ Team Sentence

❋ Comes from the Greek *syntaxis*—"arrangement"
❋ Believed by some to be a biological instinct: it comes naturally
❋ Computer programs and languages refer to syntax, too

Super hardworking, I am this team's great organizer. I arrange words, clauses, and phrases to create well-formed, well-structured sentences. It's my head for order that stops Simple Sentence from sounding awkward.

My genius lies in spotting connections between words, which I then use to create orderly word groupings. These help you make sense of the sentences you hear, speak, read, and write. Believe it or not, you know me better than you might think and can tell when I'm not pulling my weight. See, if I mess up, instead of *Joel baked a crumbly pecan pie*, you get *A baked pecan crumbly Joel pie*. Hmm . . . my fooling around has made "baked" into an adjective instead of a verb. Simple Sentence won't stand for that—I'd better get it fixed!

✓ **DO** remember that a simple sentence follows the basic grammatical order of subject-verb-object: *The girl read the book.*

✗ **DON'T** be surprised if poems jumble up syntax—poets sometimes purposely confuse word order to challenge the way we understand words.

Syntax

Clause

■ Team Sentence

* ✹ A group of related words containing a subject and its verb
* ✹ Clauses can be linked together using conjunctions
* ✹ An independent clause can stand alone as a sentence

Hail the team tactician! I put words into groups known as independent and dependent clauses. Each has a subject and its verb, but the dependents rely on the independents to express a complete thought. Confused? Try this for size: *While Simple Sentence does a pretty good job* (dependent), *I just can't wait to get my "claws" in to make things clearer* (independent).

Clause

✓ **DO** use a conjunction to separate two independent clauses: *My dad has a new car, and we're going for a drive.*

✗ **DON'T** forget to use a comma to separate a dependent clause from an independent clause: *Although I rose early, I was still late for school.*

Phrase

Team Sentence

- ✸ A group of closely related words functioning as a single unit
- ✸ Does not contain a subject and its verb
- ✸ Not always essential to the meaning of a sentence

Phrase

What's all this stuff about subject and verb? I shine all on my own without those two. The jewel of this sparkling team, I bring a little verve and pizzazz— a little creativity! I'm super slick, slipping in a *By the way,*—before Clause gets specific—*you owe me five dollars.* Oh, and I just love juicy detail: *my sister, the world's biggest cheapskate . . .* That's me, (in a phrase) *a little gem!*

✓ **DO** always follow an introductory phrase with a comma: *More than anything else, the little girl wanted a dog for Christmas.*

✗ **DON'T** forget that a phrase can come before or after the noun it describes: *The hardest grader in school, our teacher* (or, *Our teacher, the hardest grader*).

Incomplete Sentence
Team Sentence

- ✳ A broken-off part of a complete sentence
- ✳ Sometimes known as a fragment
- ✳ Often starts with a conjunction or a preposition

You wanna play to win? Then keep me out of Team Sentence! I'm a klutz and a clod and I'm bound to lose you every game! Try as hard as I might, I trip over my feet whenever I get close to that complete thought.

I like to start things off, oh yeah, but I just can't seem to finish 'em: *After Jake jumped,* for example. The fans are on their feet, mouths open, and yet the play just doesn't happen. I leave the idea hanging in the air—incomplete—and nothing drives sports fans more crazy! Certain words sneak into the game, just to lead me astray. Be careful with guys like *as, before, though, until, when,* and *while.* Known as dependent markers, these critters can spell trouble if they appear at the start of a sentence but don't deliver the goods. You have been warned!

✓ **DO** remember that words ending in "ing" are not verbs unless they have a helping word: *The rain was pouring from the sky* (NOT *The rain pouring from the sky*).

✗ **DON'T** be fooled by length. A complete sentence can be very short: *I smiled,* while an incomplete sentence might be long: *Although I smiled sweetly at my friend.*

Incomplete Sentence

Run-on Sentence
■ Team Sentence

☀ A sentence with little or poor punctuation
☀ One clause or phrase tends to run into the next
☀ Difficult to read easily, causing confusion for the reader

Being the fastest runner in a relay race is all well and good, but you have to pass the baton to win! And that's my problem: instead of handing the baton to the next in line, I keep going. I just don't know when to stop!

I leave a sentence without so much as a dash, comma, or period: *Grace ran a perfect race staying just behind the leaders at the beginning she picked up the pace later and her speed was awesome.* Exhausting, isn't it? Believe me, there's only one way to get to the end of a sentence without having to gasp for breath—punctuate: *Grace ran a perfect race, staying just behind the leaders at the beginning. She picked up the pace later, and her speed was awesome.* Team Sentence has a locker full of punctuation marks. Make sure you use them!

✓ **DO** try to identify the separate clauses and phrases within a sentence. This will help you decide where the punctuation should go.

✗ **DON'T** be afraid to read aloud. You'll pause naturally where the punctuation belongs: *Tom sat down, exhausted from running.*

Run-on Sentence

Complex Sentence
Team Sentence

* A sentence that is made up of a number of clauses
* Helps express several ideas at once or add detail
* Must have at least one dependent clause

A pro through and through, I weave independent and dependent clauses in and out of the game to create subtle and graceful, not-so-simple sentences.

I have no trouble expressing a complete thought, and I know exactly when to punctuate. Trust me, you'll get more information out of me than any other player: *Although Sam was not the best at spelling, he placed third in the spelling bee.* The most important idea here is that Sam placed third in the spelling bee. This is an independent clause that would make a perfect sentence on its own. But the opening dependent clause reveals more. Sam did well, sure, but I'm letting on that he had to fight hard to get there. Not only do I give you the top story, but also the story behind the story. I'm complex, I tell you!

✓ **DO** remember to join independent clauses together by using conjunctions: *Although Mary wanted to go to the party, she was too sick to get out of bed.*

✗ **DON'T** forget that a sentence that starts with a dependent clause must also have an independent clause: *Before you go to bed, you have to brush your teeth.*

Complex Sentence

Chapter 3
Me and My Shadow

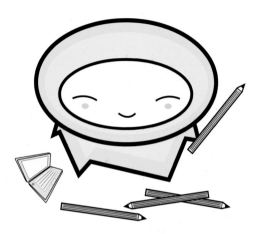

Noun and Pronoun need to be ready to change costumes at a moment's notice. For them, each new sentence is a fresh theatrical challenge. What role will they play next? Will Noun be singular, taking center stage? Or will Pronoun step out in the subjective case? Sometimes the inner drama queen takes over: Possessive Nouns and Pronoun Case are proof enough of that! Or perhaps a sentence calls for a crowd scene, in which case it's time for quirky Plural Nouns to take a bow. Whatever a sentence calls for, you should have no fear, because these guys are well rehearsed and eager to perform. Curtain up!

Plural Nouns

Possessive Nouns

Pronoun Case

Possessive Pronouns

Plural Nouns
Me and My Shadow

* The form taken when there is more than one of an item
* A number of rules govern the forms that plural nouns take
* Exceptions to the rules have to be learned

We Nouns like to think of ourselves as the leading lights of the sentence show—and why not? Trouble is, some of us insist on having an extra flourish here and there.

Take our plural forms, for example. Most of us settle for a classically simple "s" at the end of the word—*lions, toys, whistles*. However, there are some mavericks who insist on forming quirky, irregular plurals (*watches, oxen, bellies*). These wild dudes are determined to send you to the dictionary to check them out. Some of them follow the same rule (*half/halves; wolf/wolves*), but others simply refuse to play ball (*roof/roofs*). A few want it all (*dwarf/dwarfs* or *dwarves*), while a handful simply can't be bothered (*sheep/sheep*). Why? Who knows! Let's just chalk it up to artistic expression!

✓ **DO** learn the rules for plurals of "irregular" nouns—for example, words that end in "s," "x," "z," "ch," or "sh" usually form the plural by adding "es": *church/churches*.

✗ **DON'T** (ever) form a plural using an apostrophe (such as *cat's* instead of *cats*). This common mistake confuses the plural with the possessive form and is wrong!

Plural Nouns

Possessive Nouns
Me and My Shadow

* Use an apostrophe to show something belongs to a noun
* Singular possessive nouns relate to one person or thing
* When there's more than one person or thing, they are plural

There's nothing demanding, jealous, or clingy about us Possessives—we're simply little word endings that show ownership or relationship. We're impish, though, and we take devilish delight in leading you astray!

You can't outsmart us, so just learn our rules! (They're not as baffling as they sound.) We always add "'s" to the singular form of a noun, even if it ends in "s": *the class's silly behavior*. We also add "'s" to plural nouns that do not end in "s": *the women's children*. Okay so far? Plural nouns that end in "s" or "es" just get the apostrophe: *my parents' house*. Anything else would be too much! Of course, you can try to outfox us by using "of": instead of *Maude Morris's pumpkin*, you could refer to *the pumpkin of Maude Morris*. Yawn! Where's the fun in that?

✓ **DO** add "'s" to show possession in compound nouns: *the commander-in-chief's airplane*; *the mother-in-law's hat*.

✗ **DON'T** forget that only the last noun gets "'s" when two or more nouns own, or are related to, the same thing or person: *Brett and Brad's mother*.

Possessive Nouns

Pronoun Case
■ Me and My Shadow

☀ Pronouns change form depending on which case they are
☀ There are three cases: subjective, objective, and possessive
☀ Can indicate first, second, or third person, singular or plural

Remember me? I'm Pronoun, the body double that subs in when darling Noun needs to take a break. I may be a stand-in, but my range of talents far outstretches those of that loafing prima donna, I can tell you!

I step onto the stage wherever I'm needed—as subject or object of the verb, or as object of the preposition. For each new role, I alter my form—AKA my case. My smooth and subtle changes are almost undetectable. In my subjective form (*I, you, she*), I act as the subject; when I'm the object of a verb or preposition, I slip into my objective form (*me, you, her*); and my possessive form goes before a noun (*my, your, their*) or after a verb (*mine, yours, theirs*) to show possession. I do all three cases in singular and plural varieties—that's pure, can-do, multitasking genius!

✓ **DO** be careful not to get mixed up when there is more than one pronoun in a sentence: *She and I ate cotton candy at the parade* (NOT *Her and I*).

✗ **DON'T** be afraid to delete one pronoun for a minute to double-check the case: The "I" in *I ate cotton candy* is subjective, which means the "she" must be, too.

Pronoun Case

Possessive Pronouns

Me and My Shadow

* ☀ Types of pronouns that show ownership or relationship
* ☀ Sometimes sound like other words with different spellings
* ☀ Possessive pronouns never contain apostrophes

Short we may be, but sweet? Don't you believe it! Not one of us is longer than a syllable, but we can still cause trouble—lots of it.

There are just 14 of us in the entire English language. Some of us modify nouns. We express who owns or is related to a noun: *my* cell phone, *your* report card. Others stand alone in a sentence as the object of a verb or preposition: The gerbil is *mine*; let's compare our freckles to *hers*. So far, so easy, but the trouble starts when words that sound like us creep into a sentence. Take "its" and "it's," for example. "Its" is one of us, a Possessive Pronoun (as in *its devious nature*). "It's," however, is a shortened form of "it is" (*it's a disaster*). And disaster is what you'll end up with if you don't keep us apostrophe-free!

✓ **DO** stick to the apostrophe rule: *they're, it's,* and *you're* are all contractions of subject/verb forms—*they are, it is, you are.* For possession, use *their, its,* and *your.*

✗ **DON'T** confuse possessive pronouns that modify nouns with those that can stand alone in a sentence: *That is my book: it is mine; We took our ball: it was ours.*

Possessive Pronouns

Chapter 4
Friends United

Nobody knows you like an old friend, and a sentence just isn't right when the buddies in this chapter are not properly paired up. They make the art of comprehension look easy. Joined at the hip, these pals are like skilled diplomats: able to read each other's thoughts, they smooth the way so that there are no misunderstandings. Subject goes hand in hand with Verb; Pronoun enjoys a heart-to-heart with its own true Antecedent; and Modifier gets together with the subject it was born to describe. Their connections are expressed through modified word forms and endings and have their roots in the ancient heritage of language.

Agreement

Subject-Verb
Agreement

Pronoun-Antecedent
Agreement

Misplaced
Modifier

Agreement
■ Friends United

☀ Helps relate one part of a sentence to another
☀ Uses word forms and endings to demonstrate relationships
☀ Without agreement, a sentence would lose its meaning

Centuries old and craggy-faced, I'm grammar's great granddaddy. Like an ancient oak tree, the traditions of the English language have grown deep, penetrating roots. Over time I have nurtured the old family ties of agreement to tighten the connections between words in a sentence. This chapter is all about me.

I nourish the relationship of subjects to their verbs by word endings; of nouns to the nouns that they possess by word endings; and of pronouns to the nouns they represent by special pronoun word forms. These word endings and word forms symbolize the agreement between certain words. A word in isolation has limited meaning; connect the words, though, and their meanings spread and grow, just like the roots of that ancient oak. Read on . . .

✓ **DO** check all parts of a sentence carefully to make sure that all related words agree in number and gender.

✗ **DON'T** forget syntax when writing. Always group related words close together in order to avoid confusion or ambiguity.

Agreement

Subject-Verb Agreement
Friends United

✹ The subject of a sentence determines its verb form
✹ Subject and verb must agree in number: singular or plural
✹ The third-person singular of regular verbs ends in "s"

Like a pact signed between two rival nations, I am a cordial handshake between subject and verb. It isn't always easy being stuck inside a sentence together, but we've just gotta get along.

We have to stay aware of each other, even when modifying phrases and clauses try to distract us. It's all about matching or fitting in with each other. A singular subject takes a singular verb: *The violinist plays beautifully*. Plural subjects take plural verbs: *Those cupcakes are divine*. Just like you'd have trouble walking with a high heel on one foot and a biker boot on the other, your sentence will trip if subject and verb don't agree.

✓ **DO** make collective nouns (*family, team, class, group*) singular when the members act as a group: *The class wants to leave early*.

✗ **DON'T** make collective nouns singular when the members act individually. Treat the noun as plural: *The class put on their winter coats and hats*.

Subject-Verb
Agreement

Pronoun-Antecedent Agreement
Friends United

✳ An antecedent is the word that a pronoun substitutes for
✳ The term comes from the Latin word for "going before"
✳ Must agree in gender, person, and number

We're the lonely hearts of the pronoun world, always searching for our perfect match. Every pronoun has its own true antecedent, but sometimes life—and carelessly written sentences—drive us apart.

Try this troublesome sentence: *When babies cry, you are probably tired or hungry.* The noun antecedent "babies" is third-person plural, but "you" is second person—no match there. Instead use "they" (third-person plural). So, having found the right person, can you find the right number? *The monkey is a fascinating animal—they are so mischievous!* "Monkey" is singular, so a marriage with plural "they" is doomed! "It" is the solution for a match made in heaven!

✓ **DO** remember that indefinite pronouns—"anyone," "anybody," "no one," "nobody," "everyone," "everybody," "someone," "somebody"—are all singular.

✗ **DON'T** forget that "you," the second-person form of the personal pronoun, is the same in both singular and plural forms.

Pronoun-Antecedent
Agreement

Misplaced Modifier
■ Friends United

✳ A modifier gives descriptive information about a noun or verb
✳ "Misplaced" is when the relationship to its subject is unclear
✳ Can result from writing quickly, so re-read what you write

Uh-oh—watch out! I'm a real comedian, the funny guy of the grammar-error world. When a descriptive phrase (the modifier) is misplaced (put too far from what it describes), I change the meaning from sensible to silly.

My sister used a new shampoo to wash her hair, which cost $8.99. See, I'm too far away from my subject, and it sounds as if the hair cost $8.99! Avoid this comedy mix-up by placing me next to the words that I modify. Try *My sister used a new shampoo, which cost $8.99, to wash her hair.* Sometimes my subject is missing altogether and I'm left dangling: *Eating Thanksgiving dinner, the turkey was undercooked and bloody.* Ew, a raw turkey gobbling Thanksgiving dinner? *Eating Thanksgiving dinner, we found the turkey undercooked and bloody* fixes the problem.

✓ **DO** be careful with the modifiers "only," "hardly," "almost," "nearly," "often," and "even": *I almost ran two miles* is not the same as *I ran almost two miles.*

✗ **DON'T** forget to place a modifier close to its subject: *I saw a cake made with strawberries on the table* (NOT *a cake on the table made with strawberries*).

58

Misplaced Modifier

Index

Glossary

Active voice Sentence voice used when the subject of the sentence is doing the action of the verb: *I ate a banana split*. (I, the subject, actively do the eating.)

Auxiliary verb Combines with a main verb to create certain verb forms (tenses). Also known as "helping" verbs: *We will go to the party tonight*. "Go" is the main verb, and "will" is the auxiliary verb that helps "go" form its future tense.

Case A pronoun changes its case according to how it is used in the sentence (subject, object, possessive).

Complete thought Expresses a finished picture or idea. A complete sentence must express a complete thought.

Consonant A type of letter that restricts the flow of air in your mouth when you pronounce it; all letters of the alphabet except for the vowels and the letter "y": *b, c, d, f, g, h, j, k, l, m, n, p, q, r, s, t, v, w, x, z*.

Contraction One word made from two by substituting an apostrophe for letters that have been left out: in *don't* the apostrophe takes the place of the "o" in "not."

Dependent clause Contains a subject and a verb but cannot stand alone as a sentence because it does not express a complete thought.

Direct object Receives the action of the verb: *I kicked the can*. "Can" is the object of the verb "kicked."

First person Verbs and pronouns change form according to what "person" they refer to. First person relates to the self, the person speaking (or writing): *I* (singular); *we* (plural); *my, mine* (singular possessive); *our, ours* (plural possessive).

Fragment A broken-off piece of a complete sentence. Fragments do not express complete thoughts.

Gender Expresses whether a noun or pronoun is masculine (*he, him, his*), feminine (*she, her, hers*), or neutral (*it, its*).

Indefinite pronouns Refer to nonspecific people or things: *anyone, everyone, none, someone*.

Indirect object The person, or thing, indirectly affected by the action of a verb and its direct object: *I kicked the can to you.* "Kicked" is the verb; "can" is the direct object of the verb; "you" is the indirect object.

Infinitive A verb with "to" in front of it: *to laugh, to cry, to scream, to applaud*.

Inflection "Inflected" words change their form depending on how they are used in a sentence. *Write, wrote, written* are inflected forms of the verb "write."

Irregular verb Does not follow regular "-d" or "-ed" forms for past tense—for example, *bite, bit, bitten* (not "bited").

Modify When one word "modifies" another, it describes, or makes more specific, the word it modifies. Adjectives and adverbs modify nouns and verbs: *Gooey shampoo slowly dripped down the shower wall.* "Gooey" modifies "shampoo," and "slowly" modifies "dripped."

Glossary

Passive voice Sentence voice used when the subject of the sentence is having the action of the verb done to it: *The banana split was eaten by me.* (Banana split, the subject, gets eaten.)

Regular verb Verb that forms its past form by adding "d" or "ed" to the base verb form: *walk, walked.*

Second person Refers to the person spoken to: *you* (singular and plural); *your, yours* (singular and plural possessive).

Split infinitive Incorrectly separates "to" from the verb using a descriptive word: *to hungrily eat* instead of *to eat hungrily.*

Subject The person, animal, object, or idea that the sentence is about. Usually performs the action of the verb in a sentence. Complete sentences must contain at least a subject and its verb.

Syllable Pronounced correctly, the word syllable naturally breaks down into three phonetic divisions, or speech units: *syl-la-ble.* Each of these speech units is called a syllable.

Third person Refers to the person or thing spoken of: *he, she, it* (singular); *they* (plural); *his, hers, its* (singular possessive); *their, theirs* (plural possessive).

Vowel Letters of the alphabet that are pronounced in a "wide open" manner in the mouth, unlike consonants: *a, e, i, o, u,* and sometimes *y* and *w.*